THE PAPER CHAMP

THE PAPER CHAMP

ANONYMOUS ADDICT

J MERRILL

For permission requests, please contact the Permissions Coordinator at:

J Merrill Publishing, Inc.
434 Hillpine Drive
Columbus, OH 43207
www.JMerrill.pub

Paperback ISBN-13: 978-1-961475-53-3
eBook ISBN-13: 978-1-961475-54-0

Book Title: The Paper Champ
Author: Anonymous Addict

"I look at you and I see two men: the man you are, and the man you ought to be. Someday those two will meet."

— GENE HACKMAN IN *"THE REPLACEMENTS"*

CONTENTS

1

THE PAPER CHAMP

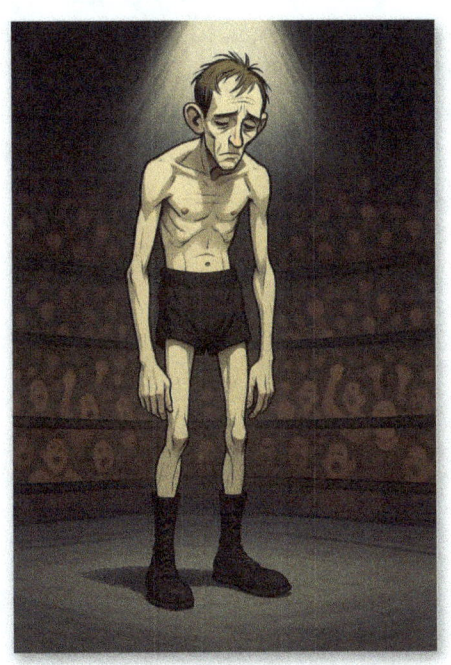

In the world of professional wrestling, the term *paper champ* refers to a champion who holds the title in transition. It is not an endearing term. It basically means the booker or promoter doesn't really know what to do with the title, so they just put it on somebody to hold while they figure out the next move. The paper champ is solid and dependable but lacks substance and any real ability to move the needle, make an impact, and put butts in seats (i.e., sell tickets).

This is a metaphor for how I have lived most of my life: glimpses of potential, signs of promise, seasons of solidness—but ultimately hollow. Continuously trying to aspire to who God wanted me to be, but falling short and getting lost in transition. Now, the why in all of this is much more complex and is a story of trauma, avoidance, and addiction. Thankfully, though, that is not the whole story. The author of my story is the Great Redeemer, and that is what He does— redeems. Redemption for man is impossible, but not for God. For God, all things are possible. All we must do is give God permission to do what He wants to do in our lives. His voice ignites a fire in our hearts that brings us back to the safest and most adventurous place in all of creation: abiding in Him.

2

BYE DAD: THE FIRST TIME

I was born in the spring of 1979 in the Midwest. My early years are mostly a blur, but there are still some moments that have stayed with me. Some are happy memories of an innocent childhood. I remember one of my first birthday parties, which was hosted at a McDonald's. Today, it might seem odd for a family to host a child's birthday party at McDonald's—but it was the '80s, and anything flew back then. I remember it as one of the happiest times of my young life. The McDonald's workers, who also acted as party chaperones, came around the corner with games and toys for my cousins and me to play with. Some adults were taking pictures with their Polaroids; others slinked back into the smoking section, spectating our enjoyment from across the restaurant.

That side table at McDonald's felt like Disneyland. The Happy Meals felt like a steak dinner. The prizes, games, and toys felt like Wonderland, and I was one of the Lost Boys, while Skip the burger flipper acted as Peter Pan each time he brought us new toys and games. It was truly a magical time that, forty-plus years later, still remains in my brain as my earliest and fondest memory. The only thing missing was Ronald or Grimace making a guest appearance—but outside of that, it was a young boy's greatest time. Not a care in the world, with Happy Meals being passed around and hot potato being played in the McDonald's booth.

The next memory that comes to me is my first trauma. I am three years old, and I am crying in my living room. I am staring out the large picture window as my father throws a suitcase into the back of his yellow-and-white Oldsmobile. He gets in the car and drives down the street as my mother pulls me from the window, tears sobbing down my young face. At the time, I didn't know where he was going or when I would see him again. It was a moment frozen in time where my young mind couldn't understand exactly what was happening— other than that it was bad. Real bad. Was this my fault? What did I do wrong? Why is he leaving me?

Turns out, I would see him every weekend or more for the next seventeen years. At the time, though, in my young mind, I felt and suffered a great loss—because, in truth, it *was* a great loss. And it stuck with me my whole life.

That trauma created a fear of abandonment in me. That fear went on to sabotage some of the best relationships I've ever had in my life—and the *best* relationship I ever had in my life: with Christ. The loss of my father in my home would be a trauma that would sneakily shape my life unbeknownst to me—but that is how most trauma works when we don't identify it, connect with it and give it to our Creator. Downright sneaky. More on that later.

3

PRO WRESTLER OR LINEBACKER

G rowing up in the '80s was truly a wild time. I know that generation after generation says that about their era of upbringing, but the '80s were something special—as evidenced by the overwhelming nostalgia that has poured out over that decade for the last thirty-five years in the form of movies, TV shows, documentaries, and even musical throwbacks. You can't convince me that *Stranger Things* would be as good as it is if it were depicted in any other decade. The '80s were something special.

My life was small, but my world was big. My connections were limited to my family, my cousins, and a few neighborhood friends—but to me, that was a vast world where I would try to find my identity and the meaning of life. Nintendo, renting video games from the store, sleepovers with neighborhood friends, playing those games, going to the arcade and movie theater with my dad, playing league soccer in the spring and fall—this was much of my early life.

My early soccer career was comical. Our coach put all the small and fast kids up front at striker and forward. Meanwhile, my buddy and I —the two largest kids on the team—played defense. We were not fleet of foot, but you really don't have to be in youth soccer. Most youth soccer games look like a mosh pit, and my fellow defender and I would just hang back. If there was ever a breakaway or a loose ball, we would waddle over. Whichever half-sized opponent approached us, we'd bully them with our size or knock them over and kick the ball to the other side of the field. We called ourselves "The Berlin Wall" (remember, it was the '80s), and I think we spent most seasons giving up minimal goals. Soccer was fun, and being a husky soccer player was also fun. It taught me early that sometimes being husky or larger than other kids wasn't a bad thing—a lesson I would sadly often forget when I got made fun of.

Monday through Friday with my mom, Saturday and Sunday with my dad. My parents were respectful to one another, but there was no genuine connection between them. There was no model for me to see every day in my young life how moms and dads love each other and love their kids daily. My parents would often give me whatever I wanted, and sadly, a lot of that came in the form of food, which led to me becoming an obese child.

I remember that my mom would take me to the doctor for quarterly checkups because of my weight. The doctor would always ask me what I wanted to be when I grew up—and the answer was always the same: NFL linebacker (he would emphasize that I had to be a Pittsburgh Steeler) or professional wrestler like Hulk Hogan. My friends and I would often watch football and pro wrestling. It was an escape for me and a dream to one day be a giant like the ones I watched on TV. I remember my family took me to a WWF show when I was young to watch Hulk Hogan take on King Kong Bundy. It was truly a magical time—watching 300-pound men in spandex and underwear body slam each other. Men with no pants battling each other for belts. I was enamored and wanted nothing more than to escape my life and become one of these titans, either on the gridiron or in the squared circle.

I remember one visit when my weight really started to climb—the doctor told me I would never be able to play for the Steelers if I didn't stop gaining weight. All you doctors out there: don't say that to a fourth grader. That messes them up in the head. I was a husky kid, and then husky turned to obese. This was also the first year I started playing football, which gave me a sense of purpose and, in my mind, helped justify my weight gain. I was a lineman, after all—and linemen were supposed to be husky, right?

I remember thinking that I was a reluctant lineman. I wanted to be a fullback, but the league we played in had weight limits for ball carriers—110 pounds—and I was about twenty to thirty pounds over that limit. Every year, I would try and fail to lose weight to carry the ball, and every year, a sense of shame and a belief that I would never be good enough grew inside me.

If you look at my pictures from sometime between second and fourth grade, that's when the weight gain really hit—and with that came the cruelty many schoolchildren endure. A lot of the cruelty came from kids I thought were my friends. It was a hard time. I cried a lot. Looking back—and here is where things come up and bite you as you get older—I never really made peace with any of this. My dad left when I was three. My weight gain. Being tormented through middle school. All of this was setting up a recipe for disaster that I would face later in life.

Now, in no uncertain terms, I would not expect my younger self to be able to identify any of this or recognize that none of it was my fault—but the older me should have. And had I, a lot of needless pain and suffering—to people I care about more than anything in this world, and to myself—could have been avoided. But again, more on that later.

My faith journey started relatively early in life. I was born into a Roman Catholic family—and where I grew up, there were only two types of Roman Catholic families: Irish and Italian. I was born into the Italian clan. Although the Irish and Italians differ in many ways, their shared sense of community, family, and culture, as connected to their faith, is remarkably similar—that, and their celebration of food and spirits with family and religion—Italians with their wine; Irish with their beer. Every Catholic school festival I ever attended as a child had these elements: food, beer for the Irish, wine for the Italians.

I became an altar boy around fifth grade. I remember thinking it was something I *ought* to do—which is how I viewed everything in my faith at the time. Right and wrong. Should and shouldn't. Like God was this silent warden in the sky, and I always wanted to stay on His good side. It's much like Santa Claus checking his list to see who was naughty or nice. I would look around at other kids getting into bad habits and use them as my barometer to gauge whether I was doing what was right and good. Good things happened to good people; bad things happened to bad people. If I stayed on the good side of things, me and mine would be fine.

This all got flipped upside down when I was sixteen.

4

FLIPPED UPSIDE DOWN

My mom remarried when I was in third grade. For the first year after they wed, we lived at my stepdad's house outside the city. I spent a year at a different elementary school—which was a tough time and, I think, a factor in my weight gain accelerating. That only lasted a short time, though, because our house in the city wouldn't sell. So, after a year—and the rural house being on the market for maybe five minutes—we were back in the city, and I returned to Catholic school with my friends in fourth grade.

My stepdad was a good man. He didn't pressure me into being in a relationship with him; he just let it naturally develop. I also remember he was much more of a disciplinarian than my mother or father—nothing over the top, but something I needed at that time in my life. I didn't know it at the time, but my stepfather was a believer in Jesus Christ.

If you're reading this book, you may or may not know what the difference is between that and being religious. Simply put, at that time in my life, I was religious. I was doing things because I *ought* to do them. It was my moral code—right vs. wrong. There was no substance, no reason behind it. Jesus, to me, was a figurehead of a belief system that had been passed down to me by my family. My stepfather, on the other hand, had a personal relationship with Jesus Christ. He was a good man—he loved my mom, loved me, respected my dad, treated us with kindness, and protected my mom and her heart.

All of this was great, but it wasn't until he faced tragedy that I saw his faith. When I was fifteen years old, he and my mom brought me into the kitchen to let me know he had been diagnosed with lung cancer. At that moment, there was a clash of doctrines I couldn't see at the time—my stepfather, facing one of the greatest battles of his life and potential mortality, clinging to his Creator, and me, thinking *everything was going to be all right because my stepdad is a good person, and bad things don't happen to good people.*

Over the next year, my stepdad slowly deteriorated, and I was oblivious and in denial. Some friends from his local church connected with him during this time. I would jokingly call them the "crazy Jesus people," but I appreciated their kindness while my stepdad was sick. I didn't think it was necessary, however, as I believed he would eventually get better. Even in the week leading up to his death, my sister and my dad sat me down to try to make me understand that he was going to die soon. I didn't believe them. I remember telling them, *He's going to be fine!*

The night before he passed, he wanted my mom and me to spend time with him. I remember being only half-present. I wanted to take a shower and get ready for school the next day. He was going to be fine. He was going to recover, and I would have plenty of time with him in the future.

The next day, during art class, my cousin, who was a senior, came and got me, bringing me down to the main office, where my mom was sobbing. My stepfather had passed. My belief system—my life— turned upside down in an instant.

I remember driving home with my aunt as she argued on the phone with Hospice to get the hospital bed out of our den. I remember driving past a church and looking at the cross, saying to myself, '*I love you anyway*,' in an almost defiant tone.

I still didn't get it.

A few weeks later, after the funeral, the "crazy Jesus people" kept coming around. My mom loved having them there. I appreciated their kindness, but they kind of weirded me out, and I would try to hide in my room. They invited us to church one Wednesday night (*Who goes to church on a Wednesday?* said the Catholic). At the end of the service, they had an altar call. It was the first time I had ever been in the presence of an altar call. They asked if anyone wanted to accept Jesus or rededicate their lives to Christ to come forward.

My mom went up. I felt weird and thought, *Good for you, Mom, but not for me.* Some old lady snuck up behind me, grabbed me by the arm, and told me we were going to the front. I have no idea who that lady was—I never saw her again. I just know I went through the motions, thought it was weird, and even had a sarcastic attitude on the way home, thinking, *Good for you, Mom, but man, that's weird and not for me.*

Again, I still didn't get it.

A few months later, a new student transferred into my class. She was a tall athlete, a stud basketball player. I had a little crush on her. Nothing huge, but I thought she was pretty cool. One day, she invited me to her home church Bible study—again, *what is with church on Wednesdays?*—but I thought she was cool, so I went along.

Over the next several weeks, the Bible was taught to me by the group's teacher, who had studied at the Moody Bible Institute. It was like a high school or college class. I remember going back each week, and my motivations shifted. At first, it was to get to know the girl, but soon, I realized I was just enjoying the class. Some Wednesdays, she couldn't go due to basketball, and I didn't care—I kept going.

For the first time in my life, I was able to read and understand the Bible. I was making connections with who Jesus was. No more silent moral police in the sky—but for the first time, the Savior Jesus Christ was present in my mind.

The moment He entered my heart was anticlimactic. After class one Wednesday, I was introduced to the Bible teacher, and his first question to me was, "So, how long have you been a born-again Christian?" My response: "I guess today?" And that was the start.

Thirty years ago—how my walk with Christ began. Almost with an affirming shoulder shrug of, *Well, sure, I guess I will.* I had no idea what I was in for or the journey that was about to begin.

5

SNEAKY TRAUMA

Whaat I thought was one of my first moments of repentance was trauma sneaking into my life that plagued me for years and set a seed of addiction within me.

As long as I can remember, I was always enamored with falling in love. At an early age, when I started noticing girls, I would get crushes and dream of what my life would be like with that person as my wife.

I took an oath one day on the playground, that if I ever got a girlfriend, she would be my first kiss, and I would make her my wife. When I got older, that belief in me evolved to whoever my first love would be my wife, and any sexual experience I would have with them would be my first and after marriage. When I was 16, however, my first kiss, and my first sexual experience, came in the form of a friend's older sister who sexually assaulted me. Now in today's culture, the idea of a 16-year-old boy being sexually assaulted by an 18-year-old girl seems laughable. To my assaulter to this day, she may scoff at that notion as well. I seemed to be a willing participant after all. Here is the truth. I was a virgin. I wanted to stay a virgin until I got married. I wanted my first kiss to be with my wife. I wanted to share all those intimate feelings with whoever I fell in love with and who would be my wife. Instead, on a random Friday night after a football game, while I was trying to sleep in my friend's basement, I was lured into a bedroom and coerced into doing things I didn't want to do. A week later, driving home from Bible Study, I wept in my car asking forgiveness for what I did - but what I did not understand in that moment - is what was done to me. I was a victim of sexual assault, and that truth would escape me for over twenty years. Instead of having that truth, the feeling of me being at fault remained. That I lost something I held dear, and I would never be good enough to have it again. That seed festered and grew over time in my life. It birthed sexual and pornography addiction that haunted and crippled me for most of my thirty years as a Christian. It ruined relationships. It ruined my marriage. How I handled the trauma and who I hurt along the way was my fault, but the trauma was not - and for anyone reading this, you will continue to struggle until you can connect with that truth. The trauma was and is not your fault. You were made in God's image. God's plans and wants for you supersede anything done to you. Do not believe what society is trying to tell you. Porn isn't normal. Casual sex is a disconnect of yourself from your soul. These things break off pieces of yourself that you lose over time. You wallow in it, the quick pleasure that leaves nothing but emptiness in its wake. I have known men, and I am one of them, that would struggle with these things for years. Praying for deliverance. Praying for it to stop. Praying for self-control. It wasn't until I identified my trauma of sexual assault, that something was taken from me, and that it wasn't my fault, that I was even remotely able to start a healing journey. A healing journey which I fouled up for the first time because a true healing journey never ends. It is continuous throughout the rest of your life, and it must be connected to our Creator. You also need to understand that until you make this connection, and get real healing, the cycle will never end. Even if you had the choice to stop – you couldn't. You will just keep drowning in the cycle.

6

BYE DAD – THE LAST TIME

I attended college, where I played football and joined a meathead fraternity. I use the term *meathead* in a lovable way. Some of those guys I'm still friends with to this day.

At this point in my story, I had been a Christian for about four years. My life was circling its first addiction cycle. The sexual assault I suffered when I was sixteen had laid dormant—until college. For much of my freshman year, I dove headfirst into sexual sin. I felt numb to it, but deep down, there was despair in me because this was something I truly wanted to save for marriage. But my trauma had me believing I wasn't worthy of that. That I had already given a piece of myself away—so what was one more? And then one more. That was how the lie worked. Disconnected from the truth: I didn't give anything away—it was taken.

Sadly, I believed the lie and continued giving away piece after piece of myself through addiction.

After my sophomore year, I got involved with the Fellowship of Christian Athletes. That summer, I served at FCA camps. It was a spiritual awakening that reconnected me to my relationship with Christ. I was back on the right path. I still hadn't identified the traumas in me or how they fed my addiction cycles. But, for the first time in my young Christian life, I was moving toward Christ with strength and clarity.

During my junior year, people started to take notice. My faith was more alive. My intentionality—both day-to-day and through football —had changed. One day, my head football coach pulled me aside and asked what had changed. All I could say was, "Jesus." Not because I didn't have a better answer but because I didn't fully understand it myself.

Those four months were a special season in my life. My only regret is that it didn't last. But looking back, that was the way the story was meant to unfold. Addiction cycles persist until you, as an individual, identify your traumas, recognize they're not your fault, and give your-self the same grace, love, and mercy God gives you.

Unfortunately, more trauma was at my doorstep.

It's early December 2000. I'm a senior in college. I just finished reviewing for a German final and am eating breakfast with one of my fraternity brothers. I'm relaxed, aside from mild anxiety—German was by far my worst subject—but as the saying goes, "D's get degrees."

I leave the dining hall and start heading back to my dorm. As I walk up the sidewalk, I see a friend running toward me. As he approaches, he yells, "Call home!" and keeps running back to the dining hall. I'm confused (it turns out he was gathering the rest of my friends), but that confusion quickly turns into dread.

At this point in my faith, I had one prayer I repeated often: "Lord, please let my dad and sister know You. If anything ever happens to them, let them have committed to You so I can see them in heaven again." I knew something was wrong. I just didn't know which one.

The walk to my dorm felt like an eternity. When I got there, I picked up the phone and called home. The phone rang. My sister's best friend answered, trying to hide her tears.

"Hello."

"What happened?"

"Oh, um, uh... hold on."

"What's going on?"

"Hey."

"What happened?"

"...Daddy is gone." (she begins to sob)

"What...?"

"He died."

"I'll be right home."

I hung up the phone, and something inside me snapped. I hurled the phone across the room. It shattered into what felt like a thousand pieces. A fit of rage overtook me—twenty seconds of pure fury. I nearly ripped the door off its hinge, stumbled into the hallway, and began destroying anything I could get my hands on.

It was 9:00 a.m. Some of my fraternity brothers came running out of their rooms. When the first one reached me, all my strength left me. I collapsed to the floor.

"My dad is dead!" I screamed, sobbing uncontrollably.

The next five minutes felt like a lifetime. I couldn't move. I wept. All I kept asking was, *Why?* Not just why he was gone but where he was now. *Is my dad truly in hell? God, why didn't you answer my prayer?*

After I dried my tears, I turned numb. I bottled everything up—for what I thought would be the next six months, but it turned out to be the next twenty-six years. I waited in the dorm lounge for my ride.

When they arrived, it was my mom—and, to my surprise, one of the "crazy Jesus people." He tried to talk to me the whole way home. Quoting Scripture and offering encouragement. I wasn't listening to any of it.

Looking back, he was doing exactly what God had called him to do. He was a roadmap to where I needed to go. But I wasn't ready.

I still didn't get it.

The next six months were a blur. I was stone-faced at the funeral while my sister grieved. I grieved alone—at night when no one could see me. That wasn't healthy. But the center of my grief wasn't just that my dad was gone. It was the terror that he might be lost forever. That has haunted me for most of my life.

Why didn't God answer my prayer?

But—and this is where I acknowledge my own fault—God did reach out to me through my sister and my college pastor.

At the time, I couldn't accept what they shared. I wasn't ready. I was still believing lies.

One day, as my sister was grieving, she opened her Bible at random, as she often did, and began reading. She landed on the story of Zacchaeus, the tax collector. Moments later, our college pastor randomly called the house. He spoke to my sister, offering comfort and reminding her that salvation is open to anyone—even the thief on the cross next to Jesus.

My sister told me all of this. I resisted. But deep down, I know the truth. God was reaching out to me. He was comforting me.

You see, my dad worked for the IRS for over thirty years. He was a tax collector.

So of all the parables, all the stories, all the random verses my sister could have turned to—it was *that* one. Followed by a phone call from a man of God. That's not a coincidence. That's the love of God.

I still miss my dad. I wish he had met my wife. I wish he had held my daughter. But I'm thankful for the time we had. And I'm grateful that *maybe*—just maybe—God did answer that prayer. Perhaps he *is* waiting for me in heaven.

No matter what, God is good. And He loves us in our darkest, weakest moments.

7

HELLO AND GOODBYE, MOM

My mother was born a twin. As I grew up, I would hear stories about how she and my uncle got into all sorts of wild adventures. The stories I heard, though, didn't resemble the mom I knew. My view of my mom was broken up into four parts.

Part One was my mom raising a young boy from the ages of three to seven by herself. She did her best. She worked full-time for the Department of Transportation. I remember her being a good mom for the most part, and, as mentioned before, she and my dad were doing their best. I also recall that as I grew older, I was unable to imagine how the two of them were ever married. My dad was super calm and laid-back. My mom was super high-strung and sometimes really dramatic. As I matured, I concluded their divorce was due to personality clashes. I was mystified how they had lived together long enough to have two kids. I was terribly misinformed, but that was my view of Mom during Part One.

Part Two of my mom was the time when she met and married my stepdad. This was one of the best versions of my mom. She was in love with a godly man who loved her back. I remember being grossed out as a kid by the affection they showed each other but looking back now, that's the stuff great marriages are made of. My stepdad was a calming presence for my mom. My sister and dad even noticed it. I think God used my stepdad to help my mom find herself again—her worth, who she was, and who God wanted her to be. She was much calmer during this time, more connected, and far less dramatic and high-strung.

Part Three of my mom was the hardest time in our relationship. This was the stretch after my stepdad died of lung cancer. She was a wreck. I was grieving in my own way—often staying up late playing video games. One night, around 1:00 or 2:00 a.m., I got up to use the bathroom. After I flushed, the water kept running—no flooding, not very loud, just a common issue. A minute later, it sounded like a bomb went off upstairs. I heard a loud crash, followed by thunderous footsteps. My mom stormed into the basement bathroom across from me, screaming and hitting the toilet. Her words were mostly unintelligible, but they were angry—blaming me for the running toilet. I stood there in shock.

Then, out of nowhere, she went upstairs, grabbed her coat, jumped in her car, and sped down the street, disappearing into the night. I sat in silence for an hour until she returned. Tears were still on my face. She came into the house and apologized.

That moment shifted everything. Her behavior continued like that. A year after my stepdad's death, she entered a new relationship and eventually married again. He was a nice man but an enabler. My mom spent money recklessly, invested in get-rich-quick schemes and gave money to all sorts of people—except her own kids. She ultimately went broke and left me with massive college debt, even though she had promised my father and me she'd cover it. She had me sign what I thought was a financial aid package—it turned out to be a student loan agreement. I should have known better at eighteen, but I trusted her.

Once, during a fit like the one over the toilet, she hit me across the face. But this wasn't little, husky me—this was eighteen-year-old me, muscle replacing fat, getting ready to play college football. I didn't retaliate. She cried. That moment solidified the shift. She was no longer the parent—I was. I became the one lecturing her. I was frustrated by her decisions. Sometimes, I isolated myself from her because of it. I'm not saying I was right, but that's where our relationship stood—until **Part Four**, which was the most important part.

Part Four of my mom began after her cancer diagnosis. I spent a lot of time at the hospital with her during treatment. At first, I was angry. *If she had just quit smoking after my stepdad died, she wouldn't be in this mess.* I had caught her hiding cigarettes so many times.

But while I spent time with her, the walls came down. We started to talk. I wanted to talk about her faith. I didn't want to live through the same nightmare I had with my dad. I needed to know that my mom knew Jesus.

She absolutely did.

I remember sitting in the hospital chair as she poured out her heart —what Christ meant to her, how He carried her through the hardest times: the verbal abuse she and her twin survived from their parents, her divorce from my dad, the death of my stepdad. As she spoke, I leaned back in my chair to hide my tears. All those years, I had judged her, not understanding she was dealing with unresolved trauma. The terrible things that happened to her created behaviors she couldn't control. But despite all that, she still walked with God— and He carried her through. My mom was and is today in heaven, a child of God.

I didn't know the truth about why my parents divorced until after she died. My belief that they were just two mismatched people was false. My dad was a gambling addict. One day, his bookie called our house and told my mom that if my dad didn't pay up by the end of the week, he'd pick up my sister from school—she was thirteen. My mom panicked, called both sets of grandparents, and somehow it got resolved. But for her, that was the beginning of the end.

I later found out from my sister that the real pain came after that. Both sides of the family turned on my mom for wanting a divorce. At dinner with her parents, they screamed at her like they did when she was a child. My dad sat silently and didn't defend her. That was her breaking point. She told my sister, "If he had just stepped up— spoken out—taken responsibility and told them to stop abusing me, our marriage might have been saved."

I love my dad, but I see now my mom endured so much trauma. That's why she was the way she was. And none of it was her fault.

But Jesus carried her anyway.

I love my mom. I'm eternally grateful for Part Four—because it revealed who she really was all along. When my daughter was born, I felt like my mom, my dad, and my stepdad were all there—watching over us as we left the hospital.

I praise God for the last conversations I had with my mom. For my sister stumbling on the story of the tax collector. For my stepdad entering our lives. For God is using him to bring me to Christ.

Also—this was the third time the "crazy Jesus people" entered my life. I call them that jokingly now. They were angels sent by God. They comforted my mom and me when my stepdad died. They comforted me when my dad died, and I shut down. And they comforted me again when my mom died.

Thank you. I'll always be grateful for how you let God use you to comfort me.

One last part about my journey with my mom that connects to the next section: just like her, I had unresolved trauma driving my behaviors and addictions.

The night my mom died, I sat in her hospice room until the coroner took her away. From there, I went and sat in a strip club with a bottle of Bud Light, totally disconnected from myself and drowning in depression.

This is because I am an addict.

8

I AM AN ADDICT

Addiction is a nasty disease. Scientists have linked it to changes in brain chemistry. One of the ugliest things about addiction is how society normalizes some of its forms. Nobody wants to be a heroin addict. People who don't have a heroin addiction look at it with either pity or contempt—but no one shrugs and says, "Heroin? Meh." Other drugs and alcoholism carry that same stigma, I think.

But food addiction? That's a different story. Jokes are made—even by food addicts themselves—while they drown in it and let it ruin their lives. Video games. Cell phone usage. These are other examples of addictions that get brushed off. "Yeah, it's an addiction, but it's not that bad."

Let's be clear: all addiction is bad—*all of it.* Addiction hijacks the nervous system, alters brain chemistry, and ruins relationships. I don't care if it's sugar or cocaine—it leads to the same end if it's not treated.

In the beginning, my addiction took the form of promiscuous sex, pornography, and masturbation. It started around my freshman year of college, three years after my sexual assault. It is crucial in my recovery to connect the dots here. My trauma planted a lie in me: that I wasn't worthy of purity, that I was dirty. That my childhood dream of saving myself for marriage had been forfeited—by me, not taken.

The truth is—and always has been—my innocence was stolen. Because I couldn't come to terms with that, my addiction cycles were activated and stayed with me for nearly thirty years.

It started with messing around in college. It escalated to watching porn and masturbating. After my dad died, it became a full-blown sex addiction. Then, there'd be a reawakening in my soul. Jesus would pull me closer through a tragedy or hardship. I'd get better for a while, but because I never connected the dots to my trauma—and because my motivation for recovery was flawed—the cycle resumed.

This was my life for thirty years. It sabotaged every bit of joy I tried to build. The lie reigned in me instead of Jesus. That lie? *I am not worthy of love.* That lie always brought me back to the mess—no matter how hard I tried, no matter how much I was loved, no matter what my motivation was.

The first time I went through recovery was because my girlfriend broke up with me. She was the most amazing woman I had ever met. Her absence pushed me toward recovery. The problem was that we got back together. We even got married. We had a beautiful daughter.

And my addiction never went away.

I hid it. I rationalized it. "I'm not watching porn as much." "I'm not masturbating as often." "I'm not telling my wife because I don't want to upset her." All of it—*total bullshit.*

The truth was, I stepped off the road to recovery because I was never truly on it. The only way to leave addiction is to do it for yourself—because God loves you, and you are worthy of love. If your motivation is anything other than this, your journey will be temporary. The lie will return. The mess will return.

That is not God's design for your life, regardless of your trauma or addiction. God wants you whole, healed, and aware of His love daily. Only that keeps you on the road to recovery. Recognizing you are walking with God *because God* is what sustains you. You are the most important thing in the world to Him. He sent His Son to die for you. That truth—that motivation—is when real transformation begins.

A wise man once told me, "People don't change when they talk to God. People change when God talks to them." *Are you listening?*

Because that's all it takes.

God is calling. He wants to heal you. He wants you whole. He wants you to live the best life imaginable—the best outcome, the best-case scenario.

But to come to this realization, I had to suffer the greatest loss of my life.

I met my wife in 2016 on a dating app. My addiction and dishonesty plagued our early relationship—but she loved me anyway. She finally had enough. As I mentioned earlier, I did an about-face, but my motivation was still flawed. I was building a relationship with the most amazing woman I've ever met on a foundation of sand—a house of cards.

We got married during the 2020 pandemic. It was the best time in our marriage. There were no distractions. We cooked together. We did puzzles together. Played games. Our neighbor would stop by sometimes, but it was mostly just us.

She was reluctant about parts of my life—especially my coaching career. She made me promise that if we had kids, I'd cut back. In 2022, our beautiful daughter was born—and I broke that promise. I justified it because I thought I was doing better. I wasn't watching porn as often and wasn't masturbating as much, so I thought I was progressing.

I wasn't.

The space left by less porn was filled with other addictions—cell phones, busyness, and one of the worst: selfishness. The more my wife pressed in for connection, the more I would raise walls and be an avoidant. I didn't feel safe with the safest person I had ever met. I would seek environments where I had some sense of control, even though that control was illusory while neglecting my responsibilities as a father and husband. I gave my wife and daughter the scraps of my life, then argued that nothing was wrong. I said evil things like, "This is my ministry. Why can't you support me?" All while she cried and begged me to stop, to be present, to come home.

Instead, I was gone. Coaching. Hobbies. Social stuff. I pushed back at her. "You need a hobby," I'd say, blaming her for her pain. I was cruel. I was absent. I was the worst husband.

And yes, I *was* evil.

Some might say I'm being too hard on myself. You're wrong. A man of God protects his wife. He loves his wife. Honors her thoughts and feelings. I didn't do that. I destroyed her.

Meanwhile, my coaching career thrived. My therapist reminds me that even in my brokenness, God was still using me—but that's still hard to accept. Who am I to question what God can do with a sinner like me?

All these accolades became reminders of what I had sacrificed.

One day, my wife told me she was done. After a weekend where I left in a snowstorm to pursue a hobby—and chastised her for not coming —I came home and apologized. But it wasn't enough.

She had had enough.

She wasn't going to let me treat her that way anymore. Maybe by leaving, she hoped I'd finally wake up for our daughter. I was in shock. All the begging, all the tears—I ignored them. And now, it hit me. I was the problem.

I've always been the problem.

My addiction had driven away the woman who loved me more than anything. For the first month, I focused on the external. I was everything she wanted me to be—but it wasn't enough. Because, once again, I was doing it out of desperation. Not out of transformation.

While all this happened, my coaching success continued. But every celebration felt like a wound.

I received many texts about the success of my coaching career. Within those texts, a group of close friends and believers reached out. Here is my response:

"If I could trade it right now, I would. I'm struggling with what the future holds. I know God has me, and at some point, this season will end. I can only pray it ends with a miracle. But honestly, every accolade, every award—it's just a reminder of what I lost.

When my wife begged me to be home, I told her this was my ministry. That God was number one, she and my daughter were number two, and everything else was number three. That was poison in already deep wounds.

I put everything before my family. That's why I'm here.

I used to forfeit time with them. Now, I'd trade *everything* for five good minutes with my wife again."

This doesn't minimize what God did through me—or the accomplishments of the people around me. Their joy is real.

But for me, all of it is a reminder of what I lost.

This is what addiction cost me. And here's the cruel irony: because of my trauma and disconnection, there was no other outcome. None of this is my wife's fault. She loved me more than anyone had ever loved me. She tried everything.

All around my life was loss and abandonment – those were the themes of my early life, and my sensitivity to abandonment led to my struggle with the defense of avoidance and space-making in intimate relationships. The crisis of my wife leaving allowed God His opportunity to bring me to a place where, by His power, I am able to overcome the barrier of self-protection.

It cost me everything. But it was the only road that could bring me here.

I have to love the man I was—the man who was a terrible husband and father. Because he is still me, and Jesus loved me then, loves me now, and will always love me.

That is my hope.

That is why I press forward.

If you're reading this and you're in an addiction cycle—*wake up.*

Tell your spouse. Tell your pastor. Find a Christian therapist who specializes in trauma and addiction. I did—and she's an angel from God. Her wisdom reminds me of the big picture—*Jesus*.

Wherever you are—it's not too late.

Wake up.

This is not God's plan for your life. Stop the pain you're causing yourself and others. Christ is the only way. He loves you. He wants you healed and whole. You are His most beloved creation.

He is reaching for you.

Go to Jesus.

THE JOURNEY
THROUGH THE DESERT

In Matthew chapter 4, the story of Jesus in the desert unfolds. After forty days and forty nights of fasting, Satan comes to tempt Him. Jesus faces three trials. First, Satan tells Him to turn stones into bread. Jesus responds that man must not live on bread alone but on every word that comes from God.

Second, Satan takes Him to the highest point in the city, tells Him to jump, and even quotes Scripture to prove He would be safe. Jesus replies, "It is also written: Do not put the Lord your God to the test."

Finally, Satan takes Him to the highest mountain, shows Him all the kingdoms of the world, and promises them to Jesus if He will bow down and worship him. Jesus answers, "Away from me, Satan! For it is written: Worship the Lord your God, and serve Him only."

When we travel through our own deserts, it's important to remember the path Jesus laid out for us. He never wavered. Even in His weakened state, He didn't flinch.

It's also important to remember that Jesus carries us through our deserts.

While I am traveling through my desert, it is sometimes hard to remember this. Far too often, I was like the apostle in the boat while the storm raged around us—helpless, terrified, and out of control.

Would my daughter never know a home where both mom and dad love each other, all under one roof? Would my wife ever be able to forgive me for the neglect that pushed her into the deepest, darkest depression? Would she ever trust that this change in me is real—and that I won't fall into another addiction cycle over the next seven years?

On my hardest days, fear creeps in like poison. Absent are the sexual fantasies that used to crawl into my gray matter and prompt me to act out. In their place now is the black sludge of fear.

Fear is like quicksand. The more you feed it, the more you sink. It tries to rob you of peace, joy, and hope—gifts that Jesus freely gives. It crawls into our minds like a worm. And if we don't hand it over to Jesus, it can cripple our faith.

As I struggled with fear, God kept reminding me that He was in charge. My circumstances—my trials—are temporary. I was to focus on each day as it came: an opportunity to let God do the good work He is doing in me.

Don't focus on your circumstances. Don't focus on potential outcomes. Focus on Jesus. Focus on *today*. Let God work everything else out.

Follow Jesus' example. When Satan comes with his weapons—don't flinch. The battleground is the mind. Focus on Jesus and what He is doing in your life.

And remember—though the battle rages on, the war is already won. Christ is King.

One day, God smacked me in the face concerning my fear. James 1:6 says, "But when you ask, you must believe and not doubt, because the one who doubts is like a wave of the sea, blown and tossed by the wind."

I've felt God speaking to me—and still, I wrestle with whether it was really Him. I struggle with being a double-minded man.

But God still gives grace. He is calling me to *believe* in what He is doing—right now and in the future—with me, with my wife, and with my daughter.

When fear hits me, I need only to keep believing in who God is and how much He loves us. When I sit in that truth, I can tackle giants and move mountains.

Knowing who God is.
Believing His promises for me.
Growing closer to Him each day.

Not letting my circumstances dictate my heart.
Letting my relationship with Christ conquer my surroundings.

I look forward to where I'll be in the future. And I pray that I can sit in His presence moment by moment—abiding in Him and taking one day at a time.

THE PAPER CHAMP TRANSFORMED

S omething I used to say a lot to try to sound important was, "There are many different ways to be great."

How I could spout that quote over and over again while living the life I was living is the pure definition of hypocrisy.

Here's the truth, though: even while I was saying that—even while I avoided and neglected my family—that was my broken self.

I've learned in recovery that I cannot hate my broken self. I have to see him the way Jesus does. Jesus *loves* my broken self. He was sending love that my broken self just couldn't receive.

I am the same person I was then as I am now. I loved my wife—even though I treated her horribly.

The difference now is *where* I am. I am still an addict. I am still the man who sacrificed his family and marriage for empty accolades. But the difference is **today**.

Today, I am connected to my Creator. Today, I'm trying to forgive myself for all I've done—to Him, to my wife, and my daughter.

It's hard because I still see—and live in—the consequences of the pain I caused. But I'm trying.

Today, I'm on the road to recovery because I love myself and believe I'm worthy of being loved.

If a miracle comes, and my family is made whole—if my wife and I are reunited again—I know God will have prepared me. If it doesn't, I will still press on because I know God wants what's best for me.

Even writing that, I struggle. Fear of the unknown—uncertainty about the future—has been one of the hardest parts of my life in recovery.

But every time that anxiety comes, I hear God whisper:

Don't worry. I've got this.

There's nothing you can do to make this situation whole.
Just focus on yourself. Get right with Me. Continue your healing.
I'll take care of the rest.
I'll tell you when to speak, when to be quiet, when to act, and
when to sit down.
I love your daughter. I love your wife. I love them more than you
ever could. Let Me care for them. You just follow Me.

> "Trust in the Lord with all your heart and lean not on
> your own understanding; in all your ways submit
> to Him, and He will make your paths straight."

> — PROVERBS 3:5–6

That's what God is saying to me. I need to listen.

I *was* a paper champ—stuffing anything into the hole in my heart
instead of letting Christ dwell and abide there.

He is what holds it all together:

Matter.
Stars.
Planets.
Oxygen molecules.
All of it.

Why do I still doubt Him? Even now, why do I hesitate to trust?

Press on, paper champ.
Fill your heart with Him. Abide in Christ.

There's a quote from *The Replacements*, a fun popcorn movie—not
award-winning cinema, but a line that's stuck with me:

"I look at you and I see two men: the man you are and the man you ought to be. Someday those two will meet."

This is my moment.

The man I was and the man I ought to be have finally met. It took thirty years.

The next thirty won't be perfect—we're all human—but for the first time, I have faith I'm on the right journey. I'm on the right path. God is walking me through this journey, and He will redeem the years.

I pray that somewhere on this journey, my wife and daughter rejoin me. But that's in God's hands.

In the meantime:

Keep pushing forward.
Keep running the race.
Keep living day to day.
Keep breathing.
Keep staying present.
Keep loving the people God's placed in your life.
Keep walking the journey of true recovery.
Keep breaking the addiction cycles.
Keep remembering your *why*.
Keep looking toward Jesus.

This is the story God is writing for you.

And it's not over yet.

Keep trusting Him.

ABOUT THE AUTHOR

The author is anonymous. I want to be clear: my anonymity is not rooted in shame. Shame is a tool of relapse. Anyone willing to put in the work and admit they have a problem needs to reject shame. I am anonymous because I don't know what the future holds. My story is just as much about my wife and daughters as it is mine. I have read a few self-help gurus that used their personal experiences, trauma, and what they did to spouses or mates - and made a good amount of profit off of it. In discussing one such author with my therapist one day - she said, "I hope he is paying for his ex-wife's therapy."

I didn't write this to sell a ton of copies. That is not the point. The point of this message is that it may find its way into the hands of someone who needs to hear it. That God would use it to help someone get in recovery. That God will use it to help someone else wake up - save a marriage - save a family - save a life from ruin.

This book is also a love letter. To my wife. To my daughter. To myself. And most of all - to God. There have been times during this when I have been really mad at God. Not because I am facing the consequences of my own sin - but sometimes life throws extra curve balls while all this is going on. I am not mad at God to forsake Him, or curse Him, or to head towards relapse. I am angry at times because I need to be honest with Him. He is my father. He doesn't want me to be fake. He wants to know me and for me to know Him. He wants me to be real.

I hope this book and its message helps you - whoever you are. God loves you.